ELEMENTAL
ELOQUENCE
BOOK
6

ISBN: 978-1-300-05657-7

1. My own making

I'm at the edge of my precipice
there's nowhere to go
no one can help me
not even a "pro"

I'm beyond redemption
I'm god's waste of time
I'm a messed up 7-up
I'm a lemon, with no lime

I can come up with soulful rhymes
that can make my heart just bleed
but, it does absolutely no damn good
if no one bothers to read

I'm through with healing everyone
I no longer really care
let everyone burn in hell
this is my soul, laid bare

I tried to get up once
it cost more than you'll know
leave me here to die
did you hear what I said, just go

don't you try and save me
from a bed of my own making
after all, what's the use
it's a worthless life I'm taking

so, before you try and heal me
by surrounding me with looney bin staff
just let me go, my way
that is my epitaph

2. Regressing to God

whoever said, "leave the past in the past"
has never had one like mine
if they spent any length of time with me
they'd know that I'm not fine

I try to be in the present, when I can
But, I can feel myself, at times, regressing
to all kinds of places that I never really wanted to go
but, it's up to me to deal with it, I'm guessing

I try my hardest, and fail at times
then sink deeper than ever into despair
I look up, while I'm drowning, for some ray of hope
something that tells me that someone does care

in the throes of my agony, I don't think about god
but I know, in the back of my mind, that he's there
I'm too wrapped up in my own pain and selfishness
to find out exactly where

sometimes he comes in glimpses of things
sometimes his presence lasts a little longer
it's up to us to realize he's always there
to lift us up and make us stronger

he's with us to deal with present things
and, he's been there for us in the past
he's the only one in our miserable lives
who's love will ever truly last

so, when you feel alone, as I have felt
and, you feel like your soul is tied and bound
just do as I do, and talk to god for awhile
for, he is always around

3. Holiday mask

there is not one single thing
I could place under the Christmas tree
that could adequately convey to you
what you really mean to me

I'd go broke buying everything you deserve
Because, one present would be just the start
So, I'm trying hard to think of that one gift
that would come from the deepest part of my heart

could I get you a case for your pillow
so you could snuggle up to it every night
could I get you a tiny bed lamp
so midnight reading can be illuminated by light

could I get you a heart shaped locket
so you could always keep a loved near
should I get you your favorite music
so you can always have something to hear

I'd really like to give you a present to remember
so, this year, I vow to give the truth
but that's one thing, I discovered, I cannot give
because, it's buried in my youth

I know you thought it'd be a sunny poem
all filled up with Christmas cheer
instead, it ended in nothing but sadness
loneliness, bitterness, and fear

'cuz, that's what's with me always
in every single conceivable way
and, it seems to always hit me the most
when we near a holiday

4. Spirit

I know I am a miracle
just because that I am here
my body will go away someday
but my spirit will never disappear

although I have gone through alot
I will never ever frown
Because, I refuse to let anything
or anyone bring me down

my spirit has much endurance
I'm in it for the long haul
even though I am somewhat short
inside I feel ten feet tall

when someone endeavors to hurt me
I just brush it aside
because, there is no one that can ever harm
the happiness inside

everytime that I am close
to getting any bad feeling
I know that that's the time
I try harder healing

many have tried to hurt me inside
to reduce me to a mass of tears
and, they don't just do it sometimes, then quit
they've been doing it for years

many have not succeeded
so, I don't know why they even try
'cuz, although I can get my feelings hurt
my spirit will never die

the ones that I have let slip through
I just have to try harder to forget
people do their darndest to dampen my spirit
but they haven't seemed to do that yet

as I said before, they never will
my spirit is something that's here to stay
and, if you start feeling good while reading this
then, you my friend are on your way

to a place I've been a long time now
where the size of my spirit will never decrease
it's a place I go inside myself
that place is called inner peace

5. Reflection

you feel you've always had it rough
you've always been looked down upon
but, tell me, what are you gonna do
when your safety net is gone

you have to stand up for yourself
mommy and daddy won't be there forever
so, when asked if you wanna give it up
you tell them all one word...never

for everyone who calls you lazy
show them what you got
for everyone who calls you stupid
show them that you're not

I had to fight for everything I got
And, you have to do the same now, too
no one gave me things on a silver platter
so, what are you going to do

are you gonna give up that easy
are you gonna turn tail and run
or, are you gonna step up to the plate
and show 'em all how it's done

are you gonna fight for who you are
and for the things that you believe
or, are you just gonna be a coward
and give up, and leave

you gotta make up your mind right now
which way you're gonna turn
are you gonna be a total wash out
or, are you gonna light a fire and let it burn

your future is yours, it's up to you
no one can tell you how to be
but, if you let others dictate how you are
then you'll wind up just like me

6. Welcome back

this is just a simple poem
to tell you that I missed you
after all, with no job
what else was there to do

I've missed you so much that
I can't control it anymore
but, here are your kids, and there's your car
let me help you to the door

I'm just joking, you've been missed
every single day
and, your kids have tested my patience
in every single way

joking again, your kids are lovely
ask me if I'm telling the truth
honestly though, I can't believe
I was ever THAT bad in my youth

even though I joke around
about not tolerating them that much
there was nothing I adored this year
more than my nieces' touch

they pulled at my heartstrings
made me want to pull out my hair
in every conceivable way possible
they let you know that they were there

and now they're back with their mother again
how will I ever learn to cope
if you get shipped out again for another tour
would I want to take them...nope

so, thank god you're back...cuz I really missed you
all joking, and kidding aside
my love, and respect for you is out in the open
and, one thing I wouldn't want to hide

I know that some of this poem
doesn't really make a lot of sense
because, I haven't been the only one watching them
most times I've been on the fence

but, the times that I've been around
must show you that I really do care
because, if I didn't, like certain other people
I wouldn't even bother to be there

but, being there for you is easy
and something that I will always do
because, sister, from my heart
I will forever love you

7. What am I

I'm the hunter
I'm the hunted
I'm the throwaway
I'm the wanted

I'm the righteous
I'm the misled
I'm the hungry
I'm the fed

I'm all things to everyone
I'm nothing to no one
I stay where I'm told
I can't wait to run

I'm the justified
I'm the misheard
I'm the seeker
I'm the lured

I'm what you want me to be
I'm nothing that you need
I'm the over cautious one
I'm the warnings you don't heed

I'm the unfocused
I'm the stare
I'm everywhere
I'm not even there

I'm the used
I'm the user
I'm the winner
I'm the loser

what am I
I don't know
until I find out
please don't go

8. Damaged normal

as a child, growing up
sometimes life hasn't treated me fair
and, I'm going to tell you about it right now
even if you don't really care

when I was born, I was damaged
there wasn't a lot that I could do
I had to adapt to my surroundings
so I could do "normal" things too

there's still some things I cannot do
and that's, kind of, ok for me
I'm just happy I'm not a throwaway kid
and, that I'm allowed to be

'cuz some treat their "damaged" very badly
some of the "normals" can be really rotten
those "damaged", from malnutrition or beatings
are locked away and forever forgotten

I've seen it up close and personal
the things that we're forced to go through
we struggle so hard, and still get ridiculed
for just trying to do things that "normals" do

so, for all of you "normals" that treat us right
I want to offer more than a hearty hand shake
for giving us "damaged" a chance to live
with situations that we didn't make

it's because of you handful of "normals"
that don't treat us like we should just be "managed"
that make me believe deep in my heart
that we aren't the ones that are "damaged"

9. Tired of war

are you as tired of war as I am
are you ready to take a stand
if you are, then join me, and I hope a few others
in peacefully raising our hand

it's so sad, and so disheartening
that we need any kind of war song
because, we all know, or at least we should
that engaging in war is wrong

I don't know why, and I don't care
what is the reason to have a nasty war
we, as a nation, should be fed up with them
we shouldn't take it anymore

to be really, truly honest
I don't really understand the need for war
has everyone taken leave of their senses
is peace such a hard prospect to ignore

I think the "higher ups" are more concerned
with all the stuff from other countries they can gain
that, instead of looking at the price it's costing us
it's ignorance they feign

they look the other way while war is happening
and are happy to reap the benefit
but, every time a soldier dies, it chips away
on the moral high ground that they sit

I can't believe I did that
I said I wouldn't open that "angry" door
but, as I stated previously
I can't take it anymore

I've never been through a war myself
but, I can imagine that it's not fun
I've seen the devastation it can cause
why do people order us to pick up a gun

fighting is not what god had planned for us
can't you all read it in the bible
why do we go on hunting and killing
we are civilized, we're not tribal

at least, I used to think, at one point in time
that we were a civilized people
but, obviously the ones running our country
haven't spent much time under a steeple

because, if they had, then they would know
god's vocabulary does not include hate
and, they need to realize that fact soon
before they condemn the world's fate

because, if they go hating and killing
everything, and everyone that they see
instead of learning to get along, it won't matter
'cuz we will no longer be

10. Afterthought

hello, my name is Afterthought
I'm not relevant in anyone's mind
in fact, no one really thinks twice about me
I'm the one that's always left behind

I'm not the first, or the last to be invited
where everyone else in the world goes
did my invitation get lost in the mail
nobody cares, and nobody knows

I'm relegated to the background scene
when they leave, nobody says bye
in fact, when they see me come in the door
they barely manage an audible, "Hi"

getting in their cars to go home
I'm right next to someone, they can clearly see
they say their farewells to them and leave
and yet, they say nothing to me

am I really that insignificant
don't I matter to anyone
sometimes, it makes me so very lonely
I feel like talking to the barrel end of a gun

I wish someone would take notice of me
cuz, when they don't, it's like I don't even matter
I feel so low on the social, and family tree
to see everyone's feet, I need a ladder

that's not the definition of an afterthought though
'cuz, eventually, they know that they're still around
it's seems, I'm more of an inconvenience
I might as well not even be found

I don't know why I even fight it
at this point, it's useless to resist
nobody pays any attention to me
I might as well not even exist

I may seem like a bit of a whiner
someone who deserves nobody's attention
but, after all, everybody is somebody, ya know
so, I believe, I deserve some kind of mention

11. Still having nightmares

I don't like between the time I lay my head down
and the time that I awaken
because, in between those two times
it's on an unpleasant trip I am taken

others have a balance of dreams and nightmares
my balance seems to have tipped the scale
no one seems to want to hear me though
and, I know I have tried to tell

I'll tell anyone who wants to listen
about the nightmares going on inside of me
but, as yet, I'm still waiting
for someone, anyone, to set me free

I've told the story so many times
but, it feels like I'm just wasting my breath
I can't have these nightmares go on much longer
because, I know they will lead to my untimely death

if you're wondering why I said untimely
it's because I think I will go crazy
no one knows the real reason I sleep so much
everyone just thinks that I am lazy

and, that's the reason I'll die from going nuts
because of everyone else's misdiagnosis
if they go on seeing lazy instead of troubled
I'll suffer some kind of psychosis

12. Done fighting

we won this round
but, we're losing the war
after all that have died
who bothers with score

we say it's for peace
and justice we fight
but, do we believe it
when we turn out the light

do you turn yourself in
when you kill a man
the armed forces say, no
because we do what we can

I'll join the armed forces
but, before I kill anyone
I'll have to say bye
my tour of duty is done

if you put a gun in my hand
then I will go AWOL
there's no way I can justify
that moral fall

there's no way I can do it
I can't take a life
I'd rather stab myself
with a blunt knife

I'll cause myself pain
before I cause other's harm
so, heed my words
and please disarm

let's live in peace
woman, child, and man
let's do it now
I know we all can

13. Acknowledgement

it's like a knife in my heart
when no one acknowledges what I do
but, the only acknowledgement I ever wanted
was acknowledgement from you

acknowledgement is very important
people need to hear what they're doing is good
if they don't, in extreme cases
they might go from nice guy to hood

as an example, I'll tell about a friend
but, no acknowledgement can hurt anyone
in any relationship, it's the difference between
I'll love you forever, and I'm totally done

I buy you a dozen roses
and show you many other affections
I'm even proud of my shrinking waist
as now I buy only you confections

but, that isn't quite enough for you
because you only acknowledge my money
and, now I've had it up to here
it's time for me to say goodbye, honey

I would have stayed if you weren't materialistic
but, that's the only message you ever sent
I was waiting, and so desperate to hear
any gesture of acknowledgement

and, so the moral of this poem goes
acknowledgement is the proper key
to be in harmony in any relationship
and, so I'm happy just being with me

the previous stanza might not have made any sense
to anyone who doesn't know
if you don't feel you've gotten any on earth
you know where your acknowledgement should go

14. Do you really know

you don't know what I've been through
so, please stop pretending
I need all your comforting
because, my heart needs mending

you can say you know all about it
you can sit there and say you sympathize
but, I know you don't know it all
so, don't tell your bold face lies

I'll sit there with you, and tell it all
if you give me half a chance
but, when I start to hint about it
you don't give a second glance

you don't really wanna hear
anything I have to say
when I'm going through the motions
you tell me "no way"

you always have something to do
and, all I wanna do is talk
but, you won't really know a thing
when all you do is walk

I have a feeling when I'm dead and gone
you will get very curious, though
and, secrets I could have told while I was alive
now you will be dying to know

so, take the chance while I'm alive
get to know every single thing
believe me, I've done it with others
I know the peace that it can bring

15. Before it's too late

there are times in my life
when I've felt very trapped
I was tired of playing along
my energy was sapped

I pretended to be one way
when, really I was another
I did it for everyone involved
including my own mother

every single bruise I took
was never physical, only mental
but I can tell everyone, right now
it didn't feel less gentle

I would have been prepared for bruises
but, with fists, I never really received any
however, mentally I received a lot
in fact, I received too many

now I sit in my room alone
not saying, "oh, woe is me"
but, because of the harm heaped upon me
it's the safest place to be

or, at least some part of me thinks it's safe
but I know, deep down, that it's really not
however, there is nowhere to turn right now
so, in here is all I've got

I know I'm in a bad place right now
someday, I hope to get out
but, right now, it's important to share
what this bad place has all been about

because, then if you are reading this
maybe you won't fall into that same hole
and, you'll be able to accomplish what I never did
that is, reaching your ultimate goal

I didn't have one, 'cuz I didn't dream
I was too busy just trying to live
I had nobody, or I didn't listen
to the wisdom that I am now trying to give

which is, never let anyone stop you from dreaming
and never let theirs distract you from yours
because, if you do that, then later in life
you'll realize you've closed too many doors

and you'll know then, way too late
that you're not where you ever wanted to be
you've spent too much time existing, instead of living
and wound up being just like me

16. Fairytale

I've been waiting every single day
for a moment to happen, just like this
the day when it all finally came true
it started when I got my first kiss

fairytales are supposed to happen that way
at least, that's what I've been told
but now I'm starting not to believe
in the story that I was sold

my fairytale of wine and roses
didn't start just like a dream
because, when my fairytale began
it had quite a different theme

I had been hurt very badly
by someone I considered close
I had to suck it up, and take my medicine
but, I was tired of that dose

now I'm looking for someone
who can take away all of my pain
I'm not looking for spectacular
I'm just hoping to feel plain

other fairytales involve love, and riches beyond belief
and, I admit, that has a certain appeal
but, my fairytale is just looking for someone
anyone, who can make me feel

because, now my sanctity here on earth
is nothing but a living hell
but, if I could find the one I described
that would be my fairytale

17. Pursuing love

I try my best to hang on to people
But, they never seem to stay
every time I turn around
it seems they go away

I try as best I can
to fit into their mold
but, I should never do that at all
or, at least, so I'm told

I should always be myself
never compromise for anyone's affection
but, that's easy for them to say
they've grown in the right direction

I've had to grow up a different way
and, love was all I ever wanted
I've always been love's pursuer
I've never been the hunted

I pursue love so intently
that, sometimes, I walk into it blind
in that way, I'm my own detriment
because, I usually find the wrong kind

and so, I've stopped pursuing it
I've resigned that, it'll find me
and, if it never does, I know
it wasn't meant to be

18. Serious poem

I feel I should tell you now
there's seriousness in what I say
but, for this subject matter
I'll mostly say it in a funny way

there is nothing you could ever do
that would make me stop loving you
I only hope, and I wish and pray
that you feel the same way too

you could knock me to the floor
you can kick me out the door
but, after all is said and done
I'd still come back for more

no amount of physical abuse
if the red cross stocks up on red juice
can ever stop me from coming back
even though my eyes might turn black

yes, it's true, we have something special
something I'd like to call, funky love
when we get married, our wedding ring
should really be a boxing glove

but, in all seriousness to what we have
together, we shall sail the stormy sea
at least until I've had the chance
to make you look like me

and, now that I've had some fun
it's time to end on a serious note
no physical, or emotion pain shall enter your life
because, on you I'll always dote

19. No confrontational skill

I live my life as best I can
trying not to make people mad
but, all that succeeds in really doing
is ultimately making me feel sad

of everybody's lack of attention
and fake, "I'm sorry", I usually get the brunt
and that is, because of one reason only
I cannot confront

if I had the balls to stand up for myself
maybe they wouldn't do that to me
but, I'm afraid that it's useless to wish
because, they wouldn't care about my plea

cuz in the end, their feelings count
and, mine don't even seem to matter
that's what drives me over the edge
and makes me even sadder

there is a lot of people that do that to you
but, it's that certain her, or him
I wonder how they'd really feel
if it was constantly done to them

but, some don't do it intentionally, though
it's just an ugly trait that they have learned
all you can do is wish that they'd been taught better
because, you're always the one getting burned

so, you better learn from all of this
you need to work on your confrontational skill
because, if it doesn't start getting better for you
it will continue, oh it will

20. Heart of stone

there's something I have to say to you
and, I admit, to you it's hard to say
but, if I don't, it's a disservice to others
so, I'm gonna do it anyway

why is it a disservice to others
because, the, "you and I", thing is through
and, if what happened to us happens to them
at least they could say they knew

you need to wake up really quickly
and realize just what you got
before you turn around one day
and, suddenly you do not

you go in and out of my life
like a relationship with me has a revolving door
I've got news for you that you're not gonna like
I won't take it anymore

you're friendly with me one moment
and in the next, your demeanor changes
I don't know if you realize this
but, that's what my definition of strange is

once it's broken, that is it
you can't sculpt it again, like fine crafted art
I'm telling you this, right here, right now
so you won't break another's heart

as well as warning people of this
so, they can beware of what you do
I'm also doing this for a selfless reason
I am looking out for you

because, maybe you don't know
how much your way can hurt another
maybe you weren't taught the same things
that I was taught by my own mother

that, if you act like a selfish person
and don't consider the feelings of anyone
then, everytime you get someone who cares
that relationship will quickly be done

because, they won't want to stick around
as long as I have for you
and, tell me, when you've exhausted everyone
what exactly will you do

I'm only telling you this because I care
and, I don't want to think about you being alone
but, that is exactly what is going to happen
if you turn your heart to stone

21. Blame me

something happened, and I don't know how
but, instead of trying to find the actual cause
everybody wants to follow a different path
the people turn to me, and pause

it seems, if only to me at least
that people are looking for someone to blame
so, they put a bunch of small papers in a hat
swish them around, then choose my name

when it seems that everyone around
is looking for some kind of scapegoat
they find the nearest person, usually me
then they all go for the throat

everyone finds a way to blame me
it's the most easiest thing to do
I bet you'd find it hard to live with everyday
if everyone was always blaming you

of course, it could just be my perception
maybe my entire thinking is wrong
but, then it happens again to me
so, I don't think that way too long

I try to avoid be blamed for everything
I really do the best that I can
But, maybe the BDM doesn't stand for my given name
maybe it stands for Blame Dat Man

I thought I'd leave this poem with a laugh
but, blame is really a serious subject
so, next time you get blamed unjustly for something
don't be like me, please object

22. The wall

there's a very huge wall between us
of which you need to be made aware
or, perhaps, you put it there in the first place
and, that's the reason you don't care

but, I do care about this wall
and, I don't think we need it around
but, I don't have the dynamite anymore
to set it crumbling to the ground

things happened in past lives
that should have never been endorsed
and, that is why the wall between us
has always been reinforced

even though the past is over
the wall grows higher every day
and, if we don't talk it over between us
none of it will chip away

even though the wall has steel around it
the inside is still made entirely of brick
so, there's got to be some way to knock it down
we just haven't found the trick

but, when we find a way to move the steel
and, we can start bulldozing the other part
maybe, we can finally find the way
back into each other's heart

23. The game

say you didn't get my message
but, is it just a ruse
am I going to be the next person
that you choose to abuse

we set out on this runway course
and, we just can't seem to stop
I don't really want to at all
but, it seems you want to hop

we came together with good intentions
we both said that we'd never leave
and, now you want to tear it down
when I am looking to upheave

so, let me know if what we have is real
'cuz, I'm not up for playing this game
but, if this is really what you want to do
then, you'll only get played the same

is what I'm thinking part of paranoia
or, is it actually right on the money
only you can answer that one, though
what is the right answer, honey

take that last line as sarcastic
or, you can take it very sweetly
but, I now feel that I have been
bundled, and packaged oh so neatly

'cuz, whether you did it, or you didn't
I either owe you the boot, or an apology
whichever way it goes, you're in the clear
because, the next move is up to me

although, I'm not up for loss of love anymore
if this is the way it has to be
I'm sorry to have to do this to you
but, no one is going to play with me

I didn't want to have to put my armor on
but, this feels just like before
after this time, I'm done with love
I can't do it anymore

but, if this wasn't a game at all
touch me with your loving hand
so I know deep down inside
that you really, truly, understand

that I was doing what I needed to do
and, I didn't mean to tear you apart
since we have a lot in common, you should know
this is how I protect my heart

24. One more chance

I've got one more chance with you tonight
one last chance to make it right
this last chance, I will not waste
I cannot plan it all in haste

I must take my time, and make it good
I'll treat you exactly like I should
it won't be like it was before
I was a fool to ever block that door

I just didn't want my feelings hurt
so, to you, I wound up being curt
and, in the interest of protecting me
I almost ruined what could be

but, I swear, this time will be much better
than the time I wrote that awful letter
telling you I couldn't take anymore
but, what exactly was I running for

in you is everything that I need
but, there was a warning I did not heed
before you start another relationship
you must be ready to take a trip

a trip to revisit your past once more
so you can finally close the door
on the old life, completely shaken
to the new one, the road less taken

but, I took the trip, and you got caught
in the vortex of my thought
and, in the words that I would say
you thought I was pushing you away

I was truly mixed up inside
and, the anger I could not hide
came spewing at you like a rejection
instead of finding another direction

now all I can do is apologize
please, look directly in my eyes
I will do all I can do
to prove, once and for all, that I love you

25. Dealing with scars

I've had quite a lot of scars in my life
not all of them were made with a knife
although there are some that you cannot see
it doesn't mean that they have to define me

I make my life what it is now
not everyone else has that same choice
some scars run deep enough to burn
I will give my scars a voice

I will let my scars tell my story
it's a story everyone needs to hear
for if you hear my scars' story
then maybe yours will disappear

but, scars never really go away
over time they do fade, though
of importance is what you do with those scars
ask me, 'cuz I really do know

some people talk about having scars
but, then you find out they're not the real deal
if you give me a chance to show you my scars
I promise, I can help yours heal

scars do not have to be a bad thing
because, they tell people that you've dealt
when you're telling how you got them, though
make sure you tell them how it felt

they need to know the worst of it
and, exactly how you got yourself out
because, then, and only then
they'll understand what dealing with scars is all about

26. Coming evil

how do I even live with myself
knowing I've done rotten things
what's the point in even pretending
god knows, I don't deserve angel's wings

I'm keeping up a good pretense though
of someone who has always done good
but, slowly there's a crack in the armor
eventually come, I knew that it would

it was only a matter of time, you see
before the evil would creep through again
no one else knew how long I kept it at bay
but, I know how long it has been

I knew I couldn't keep it up forever
soon, everyone will fully realize
that, the evil will take over completely
and, I'll no longer be in disguise

the people that everyone thought they knew
will have something else put in its place
and, when the old me finally gets swallowed whole
there won't even be a hint of a trace

the first time, I kept the evil in check
no one really experienced it, full force
but, no one knows how evil I can be
except, for maybe me, of course

27. Fearing regret, or regretting fear

they say that it's all over for me
but, my story isn't done
regardless of anything anyone has ever said
my story has just begun

they've all written me off
said that I was useless to anyone
I guess those people have no regrets at all
I know I have more than one

the one thing I regret the most
is the one thing that I hold most dear
you might think that it's strange to say
but, I regret my fear

I know I can do without it now
I hold onto it tightly, though
because, I know what would happen the very moment
I were to ever let it go

you see, fear is important to have
without it, there would be no restraint
nobody would give a damn at all
about any damage, or who it would taint

but, I know the damage not having fear could do
that's why I hold onto mine with both hands
fear and regret are closely tied together
but, I know where both of them lands

fear and regret are powerful emotions
each of them are a part of me
and, although they can be intertwined
each of them is a separate entity

28. My room

when I die
and you come to clean my room
unlike when I was alive
you'll need something stronger than a broom

my life was tidy underneath that rug
you didn't even have to pretend to care
because, unlike what you see now
there was no problem ever really there

well, at least you saw no problem
so, nobody else did either
all you needed to do was open your eyes, and ears
and, to my recollection you did neither

as I recall though, I am wrong
you saw it when you wanted to see
and, after that period of time was over
you couldn't see anything wrong with me

now that I am no longer around
you can see exactly what was wrong with me
but, I don't have to deal with the fallout of that
because, I am now completely free

you're the one who has to deal with it now
the remnants of the ghosts that are left behind
now you will be the only one, sadly
that will be driven slowly out of your mind

because, you will be looking at the pieces
glimpses of a tortured and ruined soul
and, you will finally be left to wonder
what if I hadn't let this take it's toll

29. Cupid's arrow

I don't know what I was thinking
how could I have been so stupid
she came to play, but I ducked out of the way
and, I missed the arrow of cupid

no one could really love me at all
I was doomed to a "singles" fate
I thought all were the same, wanting only one thing
I realized she was different, too late

I tried what I could to stop it from happening
but in the battle of the sexes, I wasn't winning
looking out for my heart, when she wanted to start
it seems it was doomed from the beginning

now all that has changed, it did take some time
but, I believe I finally found my true love
I know god had a hand in putting together this band
because, she came from heaven above

so, the moral of this story is very clear
if you live your life one way, and it's close to sinking
though you've known you never wanted a wife
it's time for you to do some rethinking

one last word of wisdom to impart to everyone
if you go through life not even looking for a sparrow
you know you'll find love with a beautiful white dove
because, you can never duck cupid's arrow

30. True friend

for what you do for me
I thank you very much
you are there when I happen to be
ever so slightly out of touch

out of touch with reality
but, you reel me back in
when I'm back to myself
I can finally begin

begin to pick up the pieces
when I have to start all over
when I pick up the phone, and you're there
it seems your my four leaf clover

but, a four leaf clover gives you luck
and, you give me a new life lease
when you have to talk me down
you always bring me peace

peace isn't the only thing you give
you give good advice, and laughter
a true friend is what I found in you
and, that's all I was ever after

so in my closing words to you
know I hold you very dear
even though we have our differences
I am always glad you're here

31. The day it happened

when I was born, something happened
the family dynamic got rearranged
that happens in all normal families
but, with us, something changed

I was born with many problems
too hard for you to overcome
that is why I fully understand
where your attitude is coming from

the feelings you have towards me
come from a place way down deep inside
and, although you might have succeeded
those feelings were too powerful to hide

they came out in a flood of emotion
most of them, you weren't ready for
but, those emotions just didn't stop
you kept getting inundated with more and more

the more the emotions kept coming at you
the more you allowed them to take hold
and, gone was the warmness I saw in you
in its place was nothing but cold

when I look into your lifeless eyes
I wish that I was never born
I am so sorry that I came along
and left your world tattered and torn

but, there is nothing on heaven and earth
even though I'm searching for what I can do
I know, deep down inside the very pit of me
I can't make up my birth to you

32. The journey back

I have many life stories inside of my head
thinking about them kind of got me down hearted
and, I knew I had to deal with them somehow
so, let me tell you all how it started

you have to regurgitate the bad
to be able to take in the good
plenty of people didn't think it could happen
but, I knew that it would

I knew why they had reservations
I was spending too much time going down
it must've seemed very hopeless to them
like I was doomed to have a permanent frown

I had to go very deep inside myself
although, some say I went to far
but, like I said, it had to happen
if I was ever to get to where they are

you see, it's easy to judge a person from the outside
until you've walking a mile in their shoes
then, and only then, do realize
that, yes, they've paid their dues

they've been to hell, and have returned
well, maybe not all the way
they're still struggling with their journey
but, I know they'll make it back someday

so, when you see these people on the street
and, don't worry, they're not hard to recognize
give them a pat on the back for just hanging in there
and, maybe you'll see the life return to their eyes

33. Full circle

I'm hoping you'll say yes
but, a maybe is better than a no
I'm just testing your responses
to see how far I can possibly go

I'm not trying to push all your buttons
I feel I have to test every boundary
in those moments, we clash in war
we wish each other to be sound free

free from the answers of
mom, or dad, can I
and, also free from the responses
when the parents have a prying eye

free from the condemnation
when they bring home a special friend
and, also free from the judgment
when the parent sees that friendship end

free from the angry words
that will come up in the fight
that you, and I seem to have
when I stay away all night

although you don't think I listen
I was tuned into your every word
it may not seem like I care at all
but, you have to know I heard

we all have things from our past
that our children just shouldn't know
but, I have to tell you right now
this is one place you shouldn't go

cuz I have been there once before
and now, this is my fate
I want you to really think about this
before it is too late

all the fights we seem to have
and the words I seem to loudly project
are not there just 'cuz I am frustrated
believe it or not, they're there to protect

these words I say can be for anything
not just what we're talking about here
I just want to make sure you grow up properly
before you decide to disappear

because, someday soon you'll leave the nest
and, you'll be out in the world on your own
and it's my job, whether you like it or not
to make sure you do it fully grown

and then when you're out there fully grown
maybe you'll finally come to see
that you have a child that acts like you did
and, you are behaving just like me

34. Bright side

I really don't have any idea
why I have to be this way
is it because, deep down inside
you feel that I haven't had to pay

you had it all, then something happened
it all changed the day I came along
so in your eyes, and in your mind
me living peacefully was unmistakably wrong

I had to feel what was taken from you
because, it rocked you to the core
but, I couldn't feel it as equally as you
I had to feel it more

so you devised a plan, and set it in motion
it was your most diabolical, I bet
but, I was wrong, because then came more
you weren't quite done with me yet

you played with my mind each, and every day
because, out of fear, you knew you could
and, I was powerless to do anything against it
but, happen every day, I knew that it would

I never looked for any peace of mind
because, I knew it wouldn't come
I never wondered when you would attack
I just wondered where exactly from

every day was an exercise for me
you sure kept me on my toes
but, every time that you were near
I didn't react, I just froze

now those days are over, finally
but, they replay every day in my mind
and, although I try, I don't succeed
to leave even one single day behind

but, I've learned one thing from this tragedy
and, it makes me not smart but brilliant
and that is, no matter what life gives to me now
I now I'll always be resilient

35. Learned lesson

they say it takes two to tango
I gave away my last pair of dancing shoes
I won't do it any longer
go find somebody else to use

the things you said to make me stay
were nothing but a lie
now, I'm not thinking of you anymore
it's only me, myself, and I

I will no longer replenish your spilled milk
go take it out of someone else's saucer
I should have listened to the warnings all along
all my friends said, "please, just toss her"

they said you were no good for me
they said all you would do was bring me harm
however, I convinced myself that you were different
you were as helpless as an old schoolmarm

it did take me some time to figure it out
but, when I knew what you were, out you went
it's just a shame though, that I can never get it back
cuz, I would definitely like back the time we spent

but, there's no use dwelling on it now
at least I don't have you any longer in my life
you did serve one valuable purpose though
as the best advocate for not taking a wife

although the last line of this poem is fictitious
I'll go on with life as best I can
I had no luck with any women
maybe I should find me a man

36. The prize

most people think the prize is the prize
but, it's the journey that's the prize
and we'd all be a lot better off
when that's what we finally realize

life is often very tough
no one promised it was going to be easy
but, it's when we face the hard winds of change
that often leads us to the breezy

when we happen to be dealing with a struggle
we must face up to it with dignity, and pride
there's no honor in just passing the buck
because, only cowards run and hide

the true measure of a person
is how they stand up to the roughness
do they cower when they're asked to fight
or, can they stand up to the toughness

I'm not talking about a fight with fists
I'm talking about the everyday grind
do you take each moment in stride
or, do you let it mess with your mind

life is a wonderful thing to experience
if you only let it be
don't resist what's right in front of you
I dare you all to be like me

I'm taking the bull by the horns
I'm not going to cower in defeat
because, now that I know the secret to life
my journey is almost one hundred percent complete

I've still got a long life ahead of me
I'm really not quite ready to go
but, while I'm still here, and able to speak
there is something everybody should know

when it's finally our time in life
to look back on what we've done
when we can say, look at what I've accomplished
that's the prize that we have won

37. Be glad you're gay

if I was truly gay
should I be glad that I am
because, everything that has happened
has happened because of him

it is all because of you
that I'm in a constant horny state
and, all because of you
I must learn to accept my fate

It happened on the first day
you decided to whip it out
but, it didn't stop then
you started shaking it about

I was so into it at that point
you started teasing me with every curve
you knew just how to get to me
boy, did you have a lot of nerve

I don't wanna look at you no more
I wanna play in your back door
don't pretend that you don't know
where it is I want to go

so, we did it there and then
and, you said that I was tight
but, don't worry, you'll loosen up
'cuz we'll do it every night

we don't have to limit it, though
we can even do it during the day
in fact, it makes me even hornier
so, I like it better that way

have you ever been fucked
I hear that it is fun
but, don't bother pulling out
'til all the screaming is done

cuz there will be blood
oh, yes there will
the first time is the toughest
when you try to overfill

horny people can't help it
they just want to cum
so, hope for a caring person
or your ass will become numb

but, when it is all over
and, you realize what you did
be glad that you are gay
cuz, you can't get a kid

this has been the most tongue in cheek poem
that, if you read it, anyone has ever seen
but, I'll give you points for guessing it right
if you can figure out what I really mean

38. Plea

I'm losing all control
and cannot make it stop
I was always underneath
I've never been on top

I've been there all my life
and I thought, no one must know
but, now, it's about self-preservation
so, some of it must show

I must do something fast
it's got to be something drastic
before I lose all control
and wind up going spastic

I wanted my life to mean something
or, at least have it be sweetness and light
but, through all the years I've lived this life
it seems, now, that I'm losing the fight

I still try to find meaning
even when I think there is none
I have not reached that point yet
in which I wish to pick up a gun

this is my final plea to anyone
I need you to lock me away
before I do more harm than good
please do it today

39. Accumulation

I have something to say to everyone
a little harsh, but every word is true
even though it may not encompass all
I know, there is a tiny bit that applies to you

all we are, are accumulators
we have enough, but we still want more
when we acquire it, but die in the end
what are we accumulating for

living from paycheck to paycheck
on toys, our income tax refund is spent
then, we do whatever we can, however we can
just to be able to pay the rent

there are people dying without food, or shelter
yet we spend money on a useless game
if the roles were reversed, and we were out there
tell me, would we feel the same

I'm not saying to give up your lifestyle
I'm just saying, you don't need so much
try closing your wallet, and opening your heart
everyone's price is the human touch

I know there will never be a time
when anyone says "enough is enough"
that's because, we're all just greedy humans
that means we can never have too much stuff

some have this disease more than others
and, I know I'm not completely immune
but, I'm trying to be a better person
I am trying to change my tune

are you trying to change yours as well
I hope so, for the betterment of all mankind
if we can stop needles accumulation worldwide
this doomed planet will get a much needed rewind

then, we can get to what it is supposed to be
taking care of everyone's need
instead of feeding the evilness
of the selfishness everyone knows as greed

40. Found it

I love you, but
I love myself even more
and, that's one of the reasons why
you're being thrown out my door

you've had many chances
but, you chose not to behave
and, now I have found
something you never gave

I couldn't get any
while you were here
and, now I've gotten some
since I made you disappear

it's something I was missing
for so many years
and, now that I've found it
I've finally switched gears

I've taken my life back
though, the journey was hard
I promised myself
I would not be scarred

I finally found myself
I thought I was lost
I thought the damage was done
but, there was little cost

I did fumble around for awhile
because, I didn't know who I really was
but, when you've been where I have for that long
tell me, who really does

but, now I'm back upon my feet
and, I'm ready to start over
and, it won't take any luck at all
I won't need a four leaf clover

that last part was a little corny
but, you should at least begrudge me that
because, I have learned my lesson now
I finally know where I am at

it's just too bad for me, ya know
that it took those who swore to serve, and protect
to finally force me to find what I was missing
my one, and only ounce of self-respect

41. What you took

I know what you want
and, I know who you are
you can try your very best
but, you won't be getting far

you can try what you want to try
do what you need to do
but, there's no way in hell
I will ever let this be through

what you took from me
is something I cannot get back
so, I will not rest one day, or night
until you fade to black

I don't care who does it to you
I don't even care if I'm the one
but, I don't want it over quickly
that's not the way I want it done

I want you to suffer as I have
you need to feel exactly what I feel
and, that is raised bruises all over my body
when I try to make my skin peel

I do it because I'm uncomfortable
I look in the mirror, and hate what I see
it was you who taught me not to live
all I know, now, is how to be

although, the previous line I've used before
it proves it's still inside of me
and, of one thing I am for certain
my rage will never set me free

42. Copper

I know exactly what you are
which is, a copper digger
a gold digger blows the hole wide open
you just slowly make it bigger

you take it all, but over time
so no one gets too wise
but, I know the name of the game you play
I can see underneath your eyes

I can see your very soul
I can recognize the color black
you have taken so many hearts
but, I am here to take them back

it's not only women who do it to us
oh yes, sometimes it's also men
and, we fall for it so many times
our question is not why, but when

as in, when will be the next time
and, we all know there will be one
'cuz when you're through, you move right along
you're copper diggin' is never done

so my advice to everyone is clear
be careful of every chigger
who is a man, or woman in disguise
that winds up being a copper digger

43. Memory erase

I go on like I'm ok and stuff
though, I don't think I'm emotionally well
the sad thing about all that is
I don't think my ,"loved one's", can even tell

I don't know what I can do about it
but, I want to fix it before I crack
there's got to be some way, somehow
that I can get the old me back

but, what old me do I really want
it's not like I can pick and choose
'cuz, all the ages have been unfair
so any one I pick, I lose

but, I know I can't stay who I am now
because all I am is stuck in the past
and, if there's no way to stay in present day
then I know I'm not going to last

I know there are others who feel like me
I know I'm not a special case
but, I'm pleading for anyone who has the power
to give my brain a memory erase

maybe it doesn't need to be fully erased, though
maybe the top is just full of bad dreams
when the top gets erased, the bottom will be clearer
and, I'll find out life isn't as bad as it seems

44. I am with you

what do you do with your pain and anger
when knuckles go from pretty pink to deathly white
do you just give up, and give in to the madness
or, should you finally stand up for yourself and fight

I think fighting for yourself is better than giving in
so, just calm down and assess the situation
because, giving in is the cowards way out
and, you're no coward, you're god's creation

I know sometimes that it feels hopeless to you
that you will never ever win
but, giving in is not an option
when you think about it, it's kind of a sin

because, the only way to really give in
is to somehow cause your own demise
and, I can tell you from past experience
that it is something that's not very wise

you have to think of what lies ahead
and who you'd be leaving behind
I know if you take time to think about it
I know that you'll change your mind

I know others aren't in your thoughts right now
and, sometimes it's ok to think of only you
sometimes it takes a very long time
to stop yourself from feeling blue

so, take your time, and get your head right
and get back what you have to regain
but know this, because while you are suffering
I too can feel your pain

45. Truth be told

you're trying your very best
to keep a tight lid on the situation
you know you will crack any day
as your mind swells with anticipation

I don't know how to keep this secret
it's getting harder for me to prevent
the inevitable slip up, as you learn
the truth about the main event

I kept it in as long as I could
and, I didn't want to tell you this way
but, I might as well do it now
our lives are going to change today

the person that you thought you knew
you didn't really know at all
you thought you were around for it
but, I was the one who saw them fall

the reason I know all about it
is because I experienced it firsthand, you see
because, the first time that this person fell
they happened to fall on top of me

and, I want to say right here, and now
their fall on me wasn't just a little touch
apparently, theirs was a mighty fall
because, I experienced way too much

I know what went through them at the time
had to make their existence pained
but, because of that one moment in time
mine will be forever stained

46. Who am I

taking the lord's name is vain
is nothing but pure blasphemy
bu,t to tell you the honest truth
doing things like that are a blast for me

sometimes I enjoy tearing it down
the line between heaven and hell
which just goes to show anyone
that, I'm not doing very well

or, maybe I'm doing perfect
and, this is who I really am inside
I just don't let godly people see it
so, I tell it to go run and hide

I can rip a person to shreds
without a second thought
even though that's something
that I have never been taught

I have the ability to make people mad
and make it seem like I'm unaware
when the fact of the matter is
that, I really just don't care

I can take advantage of anyone
without paying it no mind
I will never stop once to think
is what I'm doing really kind

but, then there are certain parts of me
that see that, and go to war
it's like that they have something to tell me
and, that is, what are you doing that for

those are times that I am actually good
but, they don't tend to last very long
because, right as soon as that query gets answered
I am back to doing wrong

So, I am left with an interesting question
and that is simply, "who am I"
I don't think I have heard the truth yet
so, I just listen to the lie

the truth that some do try to give
is that I am good, and I am worth it
and, the lie that tends to spread around
is that I am really not worth spit

so, I will tend to go on believing the lie
because, to me, it sounds better than the truth
after all, the truth has only been heard recently
I've heard the lie since I was a youth

47. What I mean

you could go crazy
or, choose to stay sane
either way you go
this world is a pain

there's death, and destruction
but, there's also bright spots
either one you experience
it can hurt lots

there's greedy people aplenty
but, there are many who give
after choosing one, or the other
it makes it hard to live

some are doomed to failure
some are bound to succeed
whichever way you turn
you are someone we all need

life is worth living
life ain't worth a dime
I've not decided which
so, I'll take my time

this poem is clear to some
others, not so
but, decipher it alone
because, I must go

48. Missing something

sitting down watching the tube
and, seeing the camaraderie
and, wondering silently to myself
why that never happened to me

watching it unfold before my eyes
and, feeling nothing but utter shame
friendship is something I never really experienced
but, I can't think of who's to blame

can't be me who is at fault
'cuz god knows that I tried my best
maybe it's nobody's fault at all
I just wasn't like the rest

I was forever uncategorized
it seems, I didn't have a place
no one bothered to know my name
or even see behind my face

I wasn't a very athletic person
so, I really couldn't be a jock
and, anyways, they're heavily stereotyped
they're the first that people mock

there's no way that I was the geek
because, I know I wasn't very smart
and, if you had seen my grades at all
you'd know that from the start

I wasn't really a loner either
because, loners really have no friend
and, in my lifetime I've had one or two
but, I was just a means to an end

the point I'm making is, in those groups
there were often more than a few
I just need one to stand by me like that
and, I'm crying for it to be you

49. See me

do you ever feel like someone's appendage
I mean, one that they don't even really use
just there to be a conversation piece
but, they don't sweat it if it's something they lose

I feel that way most of the time
in the doctor's office, or with family or friend
but some days, even though it'll never happen
I just wish that somehow they'd bend

see me as something more than I appear
see me for what is hidden deep
because, I can guarantee them one thing
they'll be giving up way less than they reap

but, no one talks to me like a person
they treat me as someone without a goal
however, I do have one that no one can see
and, that is to make my broken heart whole

maybe that's why they treat me like this
'cuz when my heart was broken, I was very small
so, they don't see the person that's before them
the one that has grown up big and tall

so, it's up to me to change their view
get them to see just how things are
I may have to do something drastic for them to see it
the question is, can I go that far

I'm not talking about something petty
I don't need them just to raise their heads and look
I need something that will grab them, and hold them
they need to read me like an open book

then they'll understand how it was
and they'll stop treating me a certain way
because, they'll have finally realized one thing
life is a game I know how to play

50. Crime doesn't pay

you think life is rough, and, "what about me"
so you set out to go on a major crime spree
'cuz rich is something you'd like to be
but, in that life, you can never be free

so you pick a partner like Bonnie and Clyde
then, a special place where you can both hide
you said one thing, and they're convinced that you lied
they attempted to catch you, oh how they tried

pretty soon it's clear as day
that there won't be a price to pay
and we can do it again another day
'cuz we did the crime and got away

but there really is no crime that you can do
'cuz sooner or later it catches up to you
and when you get locked up, the wronged will sue
that's when you'll find out what you blew

'cuz your days will stop being sunny
you'll have lost your freedom and money
and you'll find out what it's like to be a bunny
when they close that cell door and he calls you honey

and you will not be doing well
when big bubba's in your cell
'cuz it don't really help to yell
they have a policy, don't ask don't tell

so, before you get on the rope to climb
and even think of doing the crime
and get locked up with the filth and grime
think of how you'll be spending your time

you know that it's better just to do good
it'll be brighter in the long run, you feel that it could
it don't pay to be a common hood, be better than that
like you know that you should

51. Beyond the mask

have you ever touched pure evil
you have, if you've ever touched me
my proof of that is, several people
say that's all I'll ever be

I wouldn't want to disappoint them
Because, they have believed it for so long
I wouldn't want them having regrets
by telling them that they've been wrong

so, I'll let them think it all they want
and go on with my life as best I can
or, maybe I should give them what they want
and just be an evil man

but, should I give in to what they think
or, should I stick with what I know is true
it seems I'm stuck behind two masks
has that ever happened to you

have you been one way with some people
but forced to be a different way with others
are you nicer to your sisters
but then hateful to your brothers

how do you get beyond the mask
what exactly can you do
I say, just tear them off, and be yourself
that's the only way to know the real you

52. "Braniac" parody of "Maniac"

just a teenage girl on a Saturday night
this ain't the time of her life
she thinks she gonna be headed for a fall
she says she's nothing but lazy
she just moved to town looking for a fresh start
but all the boys they want her at night
they have all moved into the danger zone
when the lancer becomes the lance
she can cut you like a knife
when she lifts and has desire
then in fire is how is has to be

she's a brainiac
brainiac
to the core
and she's studying like she needs a higher score

she's a braniac
brainiac
to the core
I don't know what she really needs it for

on the road to straight A honor roll
is a place she longs to be
you try to kiss her beneath a tree
mess her up and she'll have a fit
you say you go together like lemon and lime
and so you have to try
you try to get her drunk while she's at a dance
but you won't make it tonight
she takes you out into the street
beats you up and takes off with the geek
don't touch, or those bruises will never mend

she's a braniac
braniac
that's the score
what did you really go out with her for

she's a braniac
braniac
there's no more
you're crying cuz your guts are on the floor

53. Friend or end

when you have a fight, you gotta know
it's not important how it started
the only thing that really matters
in the end, is how you parted

what happened during the fight
what verbal daggers, if any, were thrown
is not as important, if, in the end
you were left alone

friendship is way more important
than knowing that you were right
because, when you're hurt, and your ego is bloated
it could make for a restless night

if you manage to get good sleep
and, you weren't worried about your friend in the least
then, my friend, I can honestly say
you are nothing but a beast

because, a worried friend is a friend indeed
there's nothing worse than one who doesn't care
and, one who doesn't, is no friend at all
because, they will never really be there

so, when shopping around for a very good friend
make sure you test them out, and make them mad
because, if they get over it, and still come back
they're the best you've ever had

54. Fighting cost

you can be mad at me all you want
when you talk to me, rip me to shreds
call me all the names in the book
let everyone see your sneaker treads

when you do all of that to me, though
in the end, what did it prove
'cuz you just lost your very best friend
the situation caused me to move

you did all you could do, I know
just to prove that you were right
now I know who you really are
you could say, I've seen the light

and now you're left there all alone
'cuz there is no other friend like me
I'm what you'd call, very unique
that's all I really know how to be

I was someone you could count on
maybe I couldn't be physically there
but, mentally, and spiritually, I'm with you all the time
you could call me from anywhere

so, next time you fight, please take stock
and, please remember, I'm your friend
however, sometimes, even though you won't like it
I will refuse to bend

you probably thought I'd say something different
just by the way I set it up
but, you should know by my uniqueness
I'm always wearing a protective cup

55. Meal

you bring out the hurt
you force out the disgust
I know you don't mean to
but, I feel that you must

for, it helps me to write
and starts me to heal
this is the soup
that I use for my meal

what do I mean
this is not an entree
this is just the garnish
of what I have to say

the little sprinkles of mind
there will be more
when I venture inside
my kitchen door

although I'm not done
this is the last
I have to say
about my past

concentrate on future
is what I must do
but, I am lost
so, I look to you

but, you are lost too
that's just the deal
you are still working
on your own meal

56. Still dealing

you're done with one side, then you flip me over
as if I was an underdone pancake
just to see how much of your brand of love
it is that I can take

I took it through middle school, and on from there
I didn't raise any objection
possibly because, only out of loneliness
I was afraid of your rejection

but now it's over, time to move on
at least, that's what certain people keeps saying
and, I try my best, as hard as I can
the lord knows how I keep praying

the memories stay with me, all of the time
from them, I don't get any rest
I know all questions, and only some of the answers
but, I'm really tired of taking this test

I know, though, that the strong suffer through it
so they can help the weak break down that door
at least, that is what I have to believe
otherwise, what did I go through it for

I just hope, when I get up to god
that he really has all the answers for me
and, then I can be a good little angel
'cuz I will finally have been set free

57. Life of a petty criminal

if you have something
that I need
I don't really care
if you bleed

plus, if you have a car
I don't care what make
that's one thing
that I'm going to take

I'm a mugger, or robber
call me what you want
when I carry a gun
give me the money up front

rings, or jewelry
if you have them
I'll take everything
on a whim

the life of a criminal
is something to behold
we never do anything
that we're told

as I said earlier
jewelry. money, or cars
we'll take it all
before we land behind bars

because, us petty criminals
are begging to get caught
love and attention
is all we sought

we just went about it
in a very bad way
so, here behind bars
is where we'll stay

until we get out
and wind up repeating our crime
and, you catch us again
every single time

58. Suffering, by the numbers

I
we
you
me

I will
I won't
you say
then don't

pain is real
dangerous to show
If it comes out
everyone will know

keep it bottled up
don't let it leak
the pain that's inside
not for the week

you think they can handle
you know that they can't
you must give your life
more than a positive slant

they can't see how you live
you know that they can't deal
so, you try hard to protect
what you know to be real

but, therein lies the problem before you
unless you open your mind a tad
and let someone see inside a bit
they can't see the trouble you've had

and they won't be able to fix it
but, you know that's something they can't do
because, you have known for some time now
that the pain has been caused by you

59. My wish

we hurt, and kill, because of our differences
nobody seems to have any pride
the way we all act like savage animals
just makes me want to run and hide

I'm ashamed of our barbaric nature
sad to say, but I have it too
but, I hope, and I pray, with all my might
that I don't end up just like you

the things you say, and do to people
are nothing but evil and sinister
nobody could ever forgive you at all
not even the local minister

you say you do it for preservation
to keep everything right and pure
but, you're the one who has been wrong all along
you are the poison we need to cure

you'll go on doing what you need to do
until we put the proverbial stake through your heart
if it needs to be done, I'm willing to do it
so we all can have a fresh start

good can't triumph 'til evil dies
but, there's no way that will ever be done
because, in my honest opinion
good will never pick up a gun

good was just not born to hate
and, it's something good will never learn
and, because of that one simple fact
out of existence, evil will never burn

so we have to learn to live with evil
we have no choice but to live side by side
evil tried stamping out good, good has come after evil
complete supremacy is something we both have tried

but, we both failed in our endeavor
we have battled each other for years
and, the only place it gets either of us
is crying ourselves buckets of tears

now, I fear it won't happen in my lifetime
but, I really really wish that it would
you have the power to make peace happen, though
so, for you, I know that it could

I wish I had all of the answers
I wish I could just make everyone get along
I wish I could make everyone love one another
tell me something, is my wish so wrong

60. Reflective mirror

do you hate yourself
because, I often do
not, because of what was done to me
but, because of what I've done to you

I took a life of innocence
or, at least, so I thought
and, I turned it upside down
with no fear of getting caught

what I did had little consequence
in fact, I don't think anyone even cared
so, I got more brazen with my attitude
and, I did everything I ever dared

but, then, when what I dared wasn't enough
I started to do even more
it wasn't pretty, but let's just say
I opened the forbidden door

and, then I got slapped with reality
I got older, and realized what I'd done
now, with those memories flooding my entire being
there are days when I wish I had a gun

I make no excuses for who I was
I make none for who I am now
I just have one single question before me
and, that question is simply, how

61. Trickle-down theory

we're underage, and innocent for such a short time
it all just doesn't seem fair
older people are supposed to fill us with wisdom
but, it seems that some don't even care

they teach us things they want us to learn
not something that we really need to know
because, until we get older, where they take us
is somewhere we shouldn't venture to go

I'm not saying all grown-ups are bad, far from it
I'm just saying the young should watch who they trust
loved ones used to say be careful, as a caution
now it's not that, it's a must

for the most part, I was affected positively by elders
but, some don't often get to be that lucky
and, some of us even get that trickle-down theory
that's when the waters get really mucky

that theory I speak of could happen to you
old affects young, and then young affects another
the affected could be a distant relative, or a stranger
it could also end up being your very own brother

that trickle-down theory affects people hard
it's not like that's where they want to wallow
but, the dynamics of their entire situation
is just so hard to swallow

I know this theory, I know it well
this is something I deal with every day
but, the worst dynamic of the trickle-down theory
is, who do I make pay

I used to think that all the time
but, truthfully, I don't think that anymore
say I've mellowed with age, say what you want
I just know I've closed that door

I don't really know how I did it
by grace of god, or a really good friend
but, I know, if you can find a way to do it
make that chapter of your life come to an end

'cuz most older people don't hurt our young
their not to be looked upon as eerie
because, most of them think like us
they want no part of that trickle-down theory

62. The unknown

I have never been more confident
or ashamed of who I am
and, it started the moment I started thinking
that I was just like them

them, are those that are normal
and, have not had a messed up life
them, are those who are knowledgeable
about whether they want a husband, or a wife

I have no gender issue at all
at least, not one that I can speak of
it's a simple, and complicated matter really
I don't know who I should love

I don't know if we have to learn it
or, it's just something we automatically know
but, I do know one thing for sure, and that is
I still don't know where to go

we try to fit into a mold all our lives
someone who we are all expected to be
I don't know what anyone expects, really
because, I'm still trying to find me

I have no notion of what the world wants
because, of myself, I'm still not sure
but, once I find out who I am
then, I'm sure I'll have the cure

the cure that stops people saying
you can't be this, or, you can't be that
because, I'm sure all of us confused people
are tired of wearing a double sided hat

we're tired of acting one way for some
and then, oh no, here comes the other
so we smile, and do all we can to fit in
when inside we're just thinking, "oh brother"

I tell you all what we should do, though
when we finally get fully grown
we should run away, and start our own colony
a race of people called the unknown

63. Sympathetic game

I know, in my life
who, and what you wanted me to be
it's because, in your life
you felt you were never set free

you sat down, and explained
that your path was frozen
and that's why, in your eyes
my path was chosen

I knew it from the start
that I never had a chance
for something that was called
a normal romance

because you took that, and changed
who I was inside
and, that luxury most people have
I was forever denied

but, don't get me wrong
I'm not complaining at all
because, although others wouldn't
I sympathize with your fall

I saw who you were
and, who you are now
and, I pray almost nightly
that you'd get back there somehow

because, although both of us
ended up with a raw deal
my anger can wait
if I can help you to heal

because, you need to be well
to face the anger I spew
even though some may be misplaced
it'll all be directed at you

and, if you're not one hundred percent
by the time my rage hits
it won't be a pretty site
cuz you'll be torn to bits

and, that's the very last thing
that I want on my mind
so for now, I may not agree
but I have to be kind

sometimes that's a struggle for me
but, when all is said and done
I know one that would be a lot happier
that I never owned a gun

64. Unfinished game

I'm gonna tell you all
about a serious kind of game
'cuz I know that all of you
really feel the same

first I'm gonna let you know
there are some more out there
the final one that I'll describe, to you
may not seem exactly fair

the game of chance
is a funny game to play
'cuz a game of chance
doesn't often go your way

a game of luck
is nothing better, really
'cuz the unlucky ones
always end up feeling silly

if it were up to me
I'd play a game of skill
it always goes your way
and, you know it always will

the thing about all that is
the game of life incorporates all three
so, me getting what I really want
is only one-third up to me

but, my game is unfinished
I'm still alive and well
what will this game hold for me
I can't really tell

so, in order to really know
what my life is all about
I have to keep it going
I have to play it out

the game of life isn't for sissies
'cuz they wind up, too early, underground
this is my game of baseball
and, I am on the pitcher's mound

65. Crazy relationship

I know you want me
don't deny what you feel
how can you look at me
and deny what is real

neither of us wanted this
but, we both are to blame
so, you need to stop denying
and realize you feel the same

the moment you stop denying
and know in your heart where you want to be
is the moment you stop pretending
that you ever wanted to be free

you said, with me, you were able to feel
like you never have before
so, don't listen to those other people
I can give you more

I can give you the world you want
but, you need to really ignore them
I can give you so much love
I can offer you more than him

I don't play games for your affection
he is fake, I am real
he is just using you to get to me
that has always been the deal

I said no to him times before
that's just something he couldn't comprehend
what he thought of as his beginning
was nothing but our end

and now he haunts me everyday
he says he wants me back
the fact that he's sees you with me
makes him see the opposite of black

he's a jealous person trying to ruin us
that's why he keeps saying those things
I never promised to stay with him
if he bought me diamond rings

I never said, if he ever left me
that I would gun him down
he's just taking it out on me
'cuz I'm from the poor side of town

he knows I can't afford a lawyer
to help me fill out a restraining order
he knows that there are many days
I don't even have a quarter

so, he can do anything that he wants
and he won't ever let me be
but, don't let that stop you
'cuz I want you here with me

don't worry about him at all
if it came down to it, he can't even fight
you could beat him with one hand tied
you only have to use half your might

but, if he comes here, not wanting to fight
if he happens to bring a gun
I'll be a little crushed, but I'll understand
if your first instinct is to run

but, if you leave me out of fear
and I vow to stop his attack
will my, "by any means necessary", scare you off
or, do you promise to come back

and, the moral of that short story poem was
if started, get out quick from a crazy relationship
because, from experience, like an overdose
it leads to nothing but one extremely long bad trip

66. Loved ones

oh, I love you
yes, I do
but, nobody loves me
more than you

what you taught me
I can't say
but, I'll take it with me
every day

you guided me
when I was wrong
that's why I'm standing here
singing this song

when I was young
and you taught me right
I made sure to listen
day, and night

even when you think
I didn't hear
my ears were closed
but, my brain was near

you can rest assured that
you taught me well
even though sometimes
you can hardly tell

but, you should know
I love you too
no matter what I say
or what I do

'cuz you were the one
that was always there
when I thought
no one would care

you were the one
to wipe away my tears
and give me laughter
through tough years

now it's time for me
to close this song
I'm sorry if I ever
did anything wrong

there's one final thing
that needs to be said
before I fold my hands
and bow my head

you need to know
everything good I do
is not because of me
it's all because of you

67. Being you

your brain hasn't been working
for an awful long time now
we've been trying to re-establish a link
but we just can't figure out how

you do things, all the time
that most would consider dumb
but, during the process of forethought
somehow your brain goes numb

you went out, and reproduced
with your brain still not in working condition
let's hope that default in your programming
doesn't pass on to the second edition

every time you appear to have a single good thought
you seem to experience a brain freeze
those are the times that the rest of us
clasp our hands and fall on our knees

I have to admit though, every once in awhile
something descent creeps into your brain
but, it's always a once in a blue moon kind of thing
so it must cause you a lot of pain

I know this poem seems kind of nasty
but, the sad thing is, it's really true
I wouldn't have it any other way, though
'cuz it's just a case of you being you

68. Anger mode

there is a lot of pain, and anger inside me
and, it's ready to explode
I just hope nobody is around me
when I decide to get into that mode

that mode really isn't hard to find
it's like there's a little switch inside
and, when something, or someone, turns it on
a part of me will run and hide

so, I've never seen my anger mode in action
'cuz those are times when I really can't see
I black out when I'm in anger mode
I don't really know what happens to me

actually, part of me retains that info
so, I must be somewhat awake
maybe it's the weaker part of me that runs and hides
'cuz the stronger part is hard to take

the stronger part of me shows the weaker glimpses
a few flashes of what I did, and said
and, when the weaker side of me sees those glimpses
I become not right in the head

I know I'm severely damaged, and need help
but, no one else seems to see what I see
they all just think it's business as usual
yep, they all think that it's just me

but, I've known it's not me for a long time now
and, to tell you the truth, I'm really scared
I just hope when they finally find out
that they will all be well prepared

69. Love gone wrong

I know why you do what you do
it's because, I don't love you
I told you plenty of times before
don't you come knocking at my door

I told you no, straight to your face
when you wanted to occupy my space
how many times do I have to say no
before you get the hint, please just go

maybe I'll do something you won't expect
because, that's the only thing you seem to respect
you don't seem to respond to timid and shy, so
I'll do something more drastic to get a final goodbye

maybe you'll respond to the barrel of a gun
oh, golly gee, won't that be fun
and, next time you don't respond to my, "no", word
neighbor's will say, "was that a gunshot I heard"

but, then next thing you know, they'll call the police
and, I'll be forced into breaking my lease
cuz, you're not really worth going to jail for
so, I'll be making a quick exit outside my back door

when they get a load of you, they won't follow me
and that's when I can rejoice, 'cuz I'll finally be free
I'll be a single man, looking towards a new life
and this time, no mistakes, I won't look for a wife

70. Front page news

don't you hate when very minor stories
become major front page news
come on journalists, if we can call you that
you've got better stories to use

I'm tired of who is marrying who in Hollywood
you journalists call that front page news
when you do a disservice to your country, like that
it's the more horrific stories that loose

there's homelessness all over the place
everywhere you look, people are starving
but, when you report stupid stuff, instead of this
what legacy are you, so called journalists, carving

if you think junk your printing now is more topical
than the fact that people around you are dying
then, fellow journalists, I feel sorry for you
'cuz you, to yourself, are lying

the rest of us aren't lying to ourselves
we know there's death and destruction around
we think this should be front page news everyday
but, you keep burying those stories in the ground

leave the crappier stories to those other rags
because, that's what it seems they're there for
serious journalists are supposed to be better than that
did you all leave your morality at the door

if you're reading this, and you're reporting real news
then, you know I am not talking to you
but, if you're one of those who report nothing but crap
then you know exactly what you need to do

www.ingramcontent.com/pod-product-compliance
Lightning Source LLC
Chambersburg PA
CBHW032013040426
42448CB00006B/607